This collection is particularly close to my heart.

Firstly, as a chef, I am proud to support my colleagues, who are among the best in the world, in this adventure of the transmission of their knowledge to as many people as possible. It is important for me to organize an international community of talented artisans of flavor; we have so much to share with the public!

Secondly, as a publisher; I decided to create this collection in order to offer the best recipes by the best chefs in the world in an accessible format. I came up with it out of my desire to transfer quality content and originality. I did not want the educational aspect of the step-by-step presentation, in which lies the true value of these books, to spoil the beauty of the object.

Daniel sets an example for all chefs. After having trained with the biggest names in French gastronomy, he was not afraid to leave France for Denmark in the 1970s, and subsequently fly to the United States in 1980 and stay there.... I admire his ability to embrace the New York lifestyle without ever forgetting his roots, without nonetheless imposing them. He offers something authentic and adapted to New York without compromising the roots of his culinary identity. Guided by his passion, he knows how to constantly reinvent himself, never resting on his laurels. To me this is a sure sign that we are dealing with a great chef!

— Alain Ducasse

my BEST DANIEL BOULUD

ALAIN DUCASSE
PUBLISHING

DANIEL BOULUD

I had to make a decision, so I chose to stay in New York, which by then had come to feel like home. Shortly after, I met my business partners and we opened DANIEL on the Upper East Side. It was the place I dreamed of opening as a young chef.

How would you define your culinary style?

Deeply rooted in French cuisine with an understanding of classic technique, flavor, and taste. It always evolves with seasonal, local ingredients and contemporary techniques.

Where does inspiration come from for you?

I get inspiration from reading old cookbooks of any type of cuisine, traveling the regions of France or the world, and discovering new ingredients, flavors, techniques, and methods. That's one reason why I enjoy living in America—I always get inspired by the vibrant range of ethnicities in New York.

How do you develop new recipes?

A new recipe can come from a few directions—it can be driven by a seasonal ingredient; or when I discover a new taste; when I dream of flavor, texture, and taste combinations; or even a reinvention of a classic combination. Often, it happens in collaboration with the close culinary team I work with every day.

Which chefs taught you the most?

Gérard Nandron in Lyon, Georges Blanc, Roger Vergé, and Michel Guérard were my mentors early on. They taught me the fundamentals of classic French cuisine and also their own takes on cuisine and creativity, although they all encouraged me to find my own style. I also learned from them a passion for wine, terroir, and the virtues of smaller farmers and passionate suppliers.

Each one of these chefs contributed to who I am today but I was also inspired by my grandmother who often cooked for us. She was a true "garden to table" cook because all the food I had growing up was 100% homegrown or home raised. When I prepare soulful French dishes, I think about the great memories I have of her homey cooking, and the passion and love she put into her food.

How did you come to create DANIEL in New York City?

In the early '90s, after ten years in New York, I often thought of going back to my hometown of Lyon, but at one point

KEY DATES	*July 1969*	*1977*	*1980*
	First time working in a kitchen, as an apprentice at Nandron, Lyon FRANCE	*First job outside France, at the Plaza Hotel in Copenhagen, DENMARK*	*Came to America to work as a private chef at the European Economic Community residence*

How do you manage to run sixteen establishments in ten different cities?

Twenty years ago, I started with one restaurant and a loyal team around me who have now helped our group grow into many restaurants. I've promoted many chefs from within and built a dedicated and trusted team to supervise every aspect of the restaurants, while weighing the needs of the kitchen and the front of house with equal importance.

Today, the Dinex Group comprises operations directors, corporate chefs, a wine director, a human resources department, an accounting team, and a communications staff. They are all part of the hidden elements that guests might not see, but whose presence is felt in terms of their expertise, time, care, and attention. They teach, supervise, enhance, and maintain the consistency of our standards and our core message.

What inspired you to become a chef?

My parents were looking for a way to channel my energy, so when I was fourteen years old, they sent me to work as a kitchen apprentice, often working sixty hours a week. I was hooked.

I didn't mind long hours because I was taking on new responsibilities and learning every day. I never felt like I ruined my youth by working, even if my soccer game could use some improvement!

GOURMET SNAPSHOT

1/ WHAT IS YOUR FAVORITE CONDIMENT?

There are five. 1) Moutarde d'Orléans—between an old-fashioned and a slightly mild, sweet, delicate mustard, it goes well with charcuterie. 2) Tabasco for whatever needs a kick. 3) I love my collection of balsamic vinegars from Massimo Bottura. 4) Fresh-made harissa with garlic, spices, and peppers. 5) Indian mango chutney.

2/ WHAT DO YOU COLLECT?

Cookbooks, knives, watches, artwork.

3/ WHAT ARE YOUR PRIZED POSSESSIONS?

Old cookbooks and my great-grandfather's gold ring, which I don't wear but was a gift to my father and then to me.

4/ WHAT IS YOUR MOTTO?

Keep learning, keep improving, and keep motivating my team.

5/ WHAT IS YOUR WEAKNESS?

Being late for meetings in New York City.

6/ WHAT DID YOU LEARN FROM YOUR MENTORS?

Gérard Nandron was the diplomat of Lyon, deeply rooted in his community and well-connected to its terroir and to the politicians and businessmen who all loved him and frequented his restaurant.

Michel Guérard was a sophisticated Parisian intellectual; a poet.

Roger Vergé was an artist, a classic and creative chef who embraced Provence with his welcoming, jovial, and warm-hearted spirit.

Georges Blanc was a dreamer. I knew him when he started his business with the restless ambition to continue to build the legacy of his family's La Mère Blanc.

I learned different things from all of them by their example, and they all had the same passion for what they did.

1986	*May 1993*	*March 2006*	*October 2009*
Took over the kitchen at Le Cirque, NYC	*Opened DANIEL, NYC*	*Received the Légion d'Honneur in recognition for contribution to the advancement of French culture*	*Obtained 3 Michelin stars at DANIEL in NY*

TABLE OF CONTENTS

TABLE OF CONTENTS

THAI SAUSAGE
GREEN PAPAYA SLAW
AND BASIL FRIED RICE

24

VENISON RAGOUT
ORECCHIETTE
ROASTED CHESTNUTS AND BUTTERNUT SQUASH

32

SEA BASS
"EN PAUPIETTE"

40

PALERON
CARBONNADE
WITH BRAISED ENDIVE

76

GÂTEAU BASQUE
WITH BRANDIED CHERRIES,
VANILLA CRÈME ANGLAISE

84

GRAPEFRUIT GIVRÉ
SESAME HALVA,
ROSE LOUKOUM

94

CRISPY DUCK EGG
AND ASPARAGUS SALAD

This simple recipe is a wonderful homage to spring and a tease toward Easter with the asparagus and the eggs. It is in the style of an oeuf mollet, but instead of serving toasted bread on the side, the crispy breading is around the egg. The dressing is made fluffy from poached eggs that are blended in, and I incorporate Orléans mustard, which is a little milder and sweeter than Dijon, with an old-fashioned, grainy finish.

We make our own jambon de Paris in New York, as part of an amazing charcuterie program we developed with Gilles Verot—the renowned Parisian charcutier. On occasion, you can enjoy this dish at my downtown restaurant DBGB Kitchen and Bar. Duck yolks bring a rich flavor that goes perfectly with the savory ham and the crisp, fresh asparagus. It's the ultimate New York Sunday brunch dish with a Parisian touch.

RECURSIVE

SERVES 6 - Preparation time: 30 minutes - Cooking time: 10 minutes

DRINK PAIRING

Vouvray or another Chenin Blanc-based white from the Loire, such as Montlouis

CRISPY EGGS

- ❒ 8 duck eggs
- ❒ 2 tablespoons white vinegar (30 ml)
- ❒ 1 cup flour (132 g)
- ❒ 1 ½ cups finely ground white breadcrumbs (235 g)
- ❒ Salt and freshly ground white pepper

MUSTARD-EGG DRESSING

- ❒ 2 duck eggs
- ❒ 2 tablespoons Orléans mustard (30 g)
- ❒ 2 tablespoons Dijon mustard (30 g)
- ❒ 1 ½ tablespoons sherry vinegar (23 ml)
- ❒ ½ cup plus 3 ½ tablespoons grapeseed oil (175 ml)
- ❒ ¼ cup olive oil (60 ml)
- ❒ Tabasco sauce to taste
- ❒ Salt and pepper

SALAD AND PLATING

- ❒ 2 bunches (24 spears) jumbo green asparagus
- ❒ Colza oil, to taste
- ❒ Lemon juice, to taste
- ❒ Salt and freshly ground white pepper
- ❒ Vegetable oil, for frying
- ❒ 6 ounces thinly sliced jambon de Paris (fresh ham, 170 g)
- ❒ Fleur de sel
- ❒ Cracked black pepper
- ❒ 1 bunch chervil, washed and picked

Crispy eggs

Bring a large pot of water to a boil, add the vinegar and a pinch of salt, and set a bowl of ice water on the side. Boil 6 of the eggs for exactly 6 ½ minutes, then remove and chill in the ice water. In a small bowl, whip the remaining 2 eggs with a pinch of salt and pepper.

01

Divide flour and breadcrumbs into separate shallow dishes and season with salt and pepper. Carefully peel the eggs under running water. Pat dry and coat in the flour, then the whipped egg, and finally breadcrumbs; refrigerate.

02

If you don't have duck eggs, extra-large chicken eggs work as well.

Mustard-egg dressing

Bring a pot of water to a boil. Gently slip in the eggs (in their shells) and cook for 4 minutes. Remove the eggs from the pot and cool under cold running water for 2 minutes. Crack the eggs in half and scoop the insides into a blender with the mustards and vinegar and whir together.

03

With the blender running on low speed, slowly drizzle in the grapeseed and olive oil. Blend until the dressing is light and fluffy and season to taste with Tabasco sauce, salt, and pepper. Refrigerate until ready to use.

04

Asparagus salad

Trim and discard the woody stems from the asparagus. With a small paring knife, pick the small leaves from the spears. With butcher's twine, tie the asparagus together in bunches of four. Bring a large pot of salted water to a boil. Boil the asparagus until tender, approximately 3 minutes (depending on the size of the asparagus).

05

Using a slotted spoon, gently lift the asparagus from the pot, drain, cut, and discard the twine, and place in a mixing bowl. While still warm, toss with colza oil, lemon juice, salt, and pepper to taste.

06

Haricots verts may be used as a substitute for asparagus.

Frying the eggs

Heat a deep fryer or pot filled ⅓ with vegetable oil to 325°F (163°C). When ready to serve, roll the eggs once more in breadcrumbs and deep-fry them until golden brown and crispy. Remove and drain on a paper towel lined plate. Sprinkle with salt.

07

Plating

For each portion, on a salad plate or bowl, arrange four asparagus stalks into a ring, with the tips facing outward. Arrange slices of ham in a rosace shape in the center of the asparagus. With a serrated knife, slice off a ½-inch (1.25 cm) cap from the wider end of a fried egg to expose the yolk. Nestle the egg upright in the center of the ham and sprinkle the yolk with fleur de sel and cracked black pepper. Spoon a few dollops of mustard-egg dressing around the asparagus, and garnish with chervil leaves.

08

Leave the fat on your fresh ham slices for extra flavor and balanced texture.

OCTOPUS À LA PLANCHA
VALENCIA ORANGE AND ALMOND PURÉE

Working at the Moulin de Mougins in the south of France near Cannes fueled my passion for the cuisine of that area and inspired me to create Boulud Sud, a restaurant celebrating the flavors and cuisine of the Mediterranean.

This dish reminds me of the southern coast of Spain, with its Marcona almonds and Valencia oranges, but the seasoning leans more Middle Eastern with Aleppo pepper. At Boulud Sud, we combine the classic flavors of the Mediterranean in the best harmony possible.

Here you have tender, marinated octopus with a wonderful charred flavor from a sear on the plancha. It sits on a bed of milky almond purée, sharpened with a great sherry vinegar and shallot dressing, and brightened with fresh orange.

RECING

RECIPE

SERVES 6 - Preparation time: 2 hours - Cooking time: 10 minutes

DRINK PAIRING
Châteauneuf-du-Pape Blanc

OCTOPUS

- ❏ 1 lb cleaned octopus
  with heads left on (about
  1 ½ lbs uncleaned, 450 g)
- ❏ Salt
- ❏ 2 lemons, halved
- ❏ 1 gallon court bouillon
  (3.8 l, see p. 108)
- ❏ ½ cup olive oil (120 ml)
- ❏ 2 sprigs rosemary, picked
- ❏ 4 cloves garlic, crushed

18

- ❏ Peels from 1 Valencia
  orange

ALMOND PURÉE

- ❏ 3 cups blanched, sliced
  almonds (280 g)
- ❏ 4 ½ cups milk (1080 ml)
- ❏ 1 sachet (1 clove crushed
  garlic, 1 sprig rosemary,
  1 sprig thyme wrapped in
  a cheesecloth and tied with
  butcher's twine)

- ❏ 2 tablespoons almond oil
  (30 ml)
- ❏ Salt and freshly ground
  white pepper

SHERRY VINAIGRETTE

- ❏ 2 tablespoons minced
  shallots (16 g)
- ❏ 2 tablespoons sherry
  vinegar
- ❏ ¼ cup olive oil (60 ml)
- ❏ 2 teaspoons fresh chopped
  oregano

- ❏ Salt and freshly ground
  white pepper

GARNISH AND PLATING

- ❏ 1 cup arugula, cleaned (12 g)
- ❏ 3 Valencia oranges,
  supremed
- ❏ ½ cup toasted Marcona
  almonds (74 g)
- ❏ 2 tablespoons Aleppo
  pepper (12 g)

Octopus

Bring a large pot of salted water with halved lemons to a boil. Add the octopus; bring to a boil for 1 minute, then strain.

01

Bring the court bouillon to a boil. Wrap the octopus in cheesecloth and simmer lightly in the court bouillon for 1 hour and 15 minutes, or until tender. Set the pot aside and let cool at room temperature for 30 minutes. Strain and chill the octopus.

02

If you can find it, fresh octopus is great, but frozen will work just as well. Just be sure your octopus is not pre-cooked.

Cut the octopus into roughly 4-inch pieces. Transfer to a non-reactive container and toss with olive oil, rosemary, crushed garlic, and orange peels. Cover and store in refrigerator overnight or for at least 4 hours.

Almond purée
In a medium saucepan, combine almonds, milk, and sachet and bring to a simmer. Cover and cook, stirring occasionally until almonds are very tender (about forty-five minutes).

If needed, add more milk or water to your almonds for purée so that they stay submerged while cooking.

Discard the sachet and strain the almonds, reserving the liquid. Place almonds in a blender and purée, streaming in enough of the reserved milk to make a thick, smooth purée. Stream in the almond oil and season to taste with salt and freshly ground white pepper.

05

Sherry vinaigrette
In a small bowl, whisk together the shallots and sherry vinegar. While whisking, stream in the olive oil and add oregano. Season to taste with salt and freshly ground white pepper.

06

Finishing and plating

When ready to serve, heat the plancha or grill to high heat. Remove octopus from marinade and season with salt and freshly ground white pepper. Sear until golden brown on all sides.

For each serving, place a spoonful of almond purée on the bottom of an appetizer bowl or plate. Top with several pieces of seared octopus. In a medium bowl, toss arugula and oranges in sherry vinaigrette to taste and arrange on top. Drizzle extra vinaigrette over top and around the octopus. Sprinkle with toasted almonds and Aleppo pepper and serve immediately.

THAI SAUSAGE
GREEN PAPAYA SLAW AND BASIL FRIED RICE

DBGB Kitchen and Bar, my most casual restaurant in New York, is a cross between a French brasserie and an American tavern, with a great selection of microbrew beers and sausages from around the world. This Asian-themed sausage was inspired by a friend's family recipe from Northern Thailand. It's light, refreshing, spicy, complex, has a unique seasoning, and a long finish on the palate.

This sausage with fried rice really takes you on a journey to the street corners of Bangkok, with the hawkers peddling their food flavored with ginger, lemongrass, curry, kaffir lime, green papaya, Thai bird chili, and popular Sriracha sauce. It's a real symphony with such a concentration of flavors.

Normally in a fried rice you find a thin, shredded crepe omelet but here we top it with a sunny-side up quail egg so you can toss the runny yolk into the fried rice.

RECICE

SERVES 10 to 12 · Preparation time: 2 hours · Cooking time: 15 minutes

DRINK PAIRING
German Mosel Spätlese

GREEN PAPAYA SLAW

- ❏ 3 cups finely julienned green papaya (282 g)
- ❏ ½ cup and 3 tablespoons lime juice (143 g)
- ❏ ¼ cup and 1 tablespoon fish sauce (75 ml)
- ❏ 3 tablespoons sugar (40 g)
- ❏ 4 cloves of garlic, chopped
- ❏ 4 scallions, sliced
- ❏ ¼ cup chiffonade cilantro (8 g)
- ❏ 2 Thai bird chilis, thinly sliced

THAI SAUSAGE

- ❏ 2 lbs, 3 oz pork belly, skin removed and cut in large dice (1 kg)

- ❏ 1 teaspoon freshly ground white pepper (2 g)
- ❏ 1 tablespoon and ½ teaspoon salt (20 g)
- ❏ ⅛ teaspoon fresh kaffir lime leaf, vein removed, chopped very fine
- ❏ 1 packed teaspoon fresh lemongrass, finely grated on a microplane (5 g)
- ❏ ½ teaspoon fresh ginger, finely grated on a microplane (4 g)
- ❏ 1 ½ teaspoons red curry paste (10 g)
- ❏ ¾ teaspoon dried tumeric (2 g)
- ❏ ¾ teaspoon chili powder (2 g)
- ❏ 1 teaspoon soy sauce (5 ml)

- ❏ Hog sausage casing, 24/26 mm diameter, rinsed well

JASMINE RICE

- ❏ 1 ½ cups jasmine rice (258 g)
- ❏ 1 ½ cups water (340 g)
- ❏ 1 shallot, sliced
- ❏ 1 garlic clove, sliced
- ❏ 1 kaffir lime leaf
- ❏ 1 teaspoon salt (6 g)

BASIL FRIED RICE

- ❏ Cooked jasmine rice, from above
- ❏ 2 tablespoons olive oil (30 ml)
- ❏ 1 tablespoon ginger, finely grated on a microplane (24 g)

- ❏ 1 shallot, minced
- ❏ 3 Roma tomatoes, concassée
- ❏ 4 leaves each basil, mint, Thai basil, chopped
- ❏ 2 sprigs cilantro, leaves chopped
- ❏ ½ tablespoon golden mountain seasoning (2.5 ml)

GARNISH AND PLATING

- ❏ Olive oil, as needed
- ❏ 1 dozen quail eggs
- ❏ Basil, mint, cilantro and Thai basil leaves
- ❏ Sriracha sauce, optional
- ❏ ⅓ cup chopped peanuts (45 g)

Green papaya slaw

Combine the lime juice, fish sauce, sugar, and garlic in a small saucepan and bring to a simmer. Once the sugar is dissolved, remove from the heat and cool.

01

In a bowl, combine papaya, scallion, cilantro, and chilis. Pour the liquid over top and marinate chilled at least one day, or up to two weeks.

02

Thaï sausage

Toss all ingredients until well combined, cover, and marinate overnight.

Pass the mixture through a coarse grind dye on a chilled meat grinder. Chill meat well.

To achieve the correct texture on your sausage, make sure all ingredients and equipment are very well chilled before preparing.

Stuff the ground meat into the casing with a sausage stuffing machine and twist into 5-inch (13-cm) long links.

Jasmine rice

Rinse the jasmine rice under cold water until it runs clear. Combine all ingredients in a saucepan, and bring to a simmer. Reduce heat to a light simmer, cover and cook for 20 minutes. Remove from the heat and rest for 10 minutes. Pour rice onto a tray with parchment paper and fluff with a fork. Cool the rice until the grains are firm.

06

Basil fried rice

In a large wok or sauté pan over medium high heat, heat the oil. Add the ginger and shallot and cook, stirring until fragrant. Add the tomatoes and toss. Add rice and allow to crisp a bit on the bottom of the pan. Toss in the herbs and golden mountain seasoning.

07

Plating

For each serving, heat a thin layer of oil in a small sauté pan, sear the sausage until cooked through, and fry the quail egg sunny side up. Plate the rice using a ring mold, and place a fried quail egg on top. Place a spoonful of papaya slaw on the side with two seared sausages on top. Garnish with the herbs and Sriracha sauce, and sprinkle with peanuts.

08

For a nice brunch dish, use a regular chicken egg if you can't find quail.

VENISON RAGOUT ORECCHIETTE
ROASTED CHESTNUTS AND BUTTERNUT SQUASH

At db bistro moderne, my midtown Parisian-style bistro, I always like the menu to have a seasonal pasta where the meat, sauce, and pasta are all in tune. This recipe is a classic for the fall and is like a fortified version of Bolognese with the wonderful flavor of venison. Make sure to sear the pieces of meat before marinating and grinding. This way the sauce gets a nice roasted flavor and is not too gamey.

Using venison is an inexpensive way of incorporating delicious game meat into your menu, but you can also substitute lamb or beef if you wish. Orecchiette is made of only flour and water, so it has a great chewiness and bite. It is the perfect pasta because it's easy to make; it doesn't require a machine, you don't have to be an expert to do it, and the little thumbprint cup you create in the dough perfectly captures the venison ragout.

RECECIPE

SERVES 6 - Preparation time: 1½ hours - Cooking time: 30 minutes

DRINK PAIRING

Piedmontese Nebbiolo such as Barolo, Gattinara, or Nebbiolo Rosso

ORECCHIETTE DOUGH

- ❐ 2 cups "oo" fine pasta flour (294 g)
- ❐ 1 cup fine semolina flour (178 g)
- ❐ 2 teaspoons salt (12 g)
- ❐ 1 cup cold water (240 ml)

VENISON RAGOUT

- ❐ 1 lb venison stew meat, cut in 1-inch (2.5 cm) pieces (454 g)
- ❐ 1 lb pork butt, cut in 1-inch pieces (454 g)
- ❐ Salt and freshly ground white pepper

- ❐ Olive oil, as needed
- ❐ 1 cup dry red wine (240 ml)
- ❐ ½ cup dry white wine (120 ml)
- ❐ ¼ teaspoon ground cloves (2 g)
- ❐ 1 stalk celery, cut into ¼-inch (0.75 cm) dice
- ❐ 1 small carrot, cut into ¼-inch (0.75 cm) dice
- ❐ 1 small onion, cut into ¼-inch (0.75 cm) dice
- ❐ 3 cloves of garlic, cloves separated, peeled and finely chopped
- ❐ ½ cup canned tomato purée (122 g)
- ❐ 2 sprigs sage, leaves only, chopped

- ❐ 1 sprig rosemary, leaves only, finely chopped
- ❐ 1 pinch red pepper flakes
- ❐ 3 cups veal stock (720 ml, see p. 109)
- ❐ ¾ cup whole milk (180 ml)
- ❐ ¾ cup heavy cream (180 ml)
- ❐ ½ cup freshly grated Parmesan cheese (20 g)

GARNISH AND PLATING

- ❐ ¼ cup extra-virgin olive oil (60 ml)
- ❐ ½ lb trumpet royale mushrooms, trimmed and cut into ¼-inch (0.75 cm) dice (227 g)

- ❐ ¼ lb peeled fresh, vacuum-sealed, or bottled chestnuts, quartered (113 g)
- ❐ ¼ lb butternut squash, peeled, seeded and cut into ¼-inch (0.75 cm) dice (113 g)
- ❐ Salt and freshly ground white pepper
- ❐ Veal stock, as needed (see p. 109)
- ❐ 1 bunch flat-leaf parsley, leaves only, chopped
- ❐ Shaved Parmesan
- ❐ Crispy sage leaves (see p. 108)

Pasta dough

In a large bowl, stir together the flours and salt. Transfer to a clean work surface and form a well in the center. Add the water to the well and, with a fork, gradually stir to incorporate the flour from the outside in.

Once the dough begins to form, knead the dough until smooth and elastic. Wrap the dough in plastic wrap and refrigerate for at least 2 hours or overnight.

01

02

Cut off ⅛th of the dough and roll on a lightly floured cutting board to create a ½-inch (1.25 cm) wide rope. With a sharp knife, cut the rope into ½-inch (1.25 cm) pieces, separating pieces as cut so they are no longer touching.

03

You can make the ragout up to three days in advance: It gets more delicious the longer the flavors marry together, but be sure to add the dairy, pasta, and vegetables at the last minute.

Lightly toss the cut pieces with a little semolina flour. Put each cut piece of dough, cut side down, on the cutting board and flatten into a disc with your thumb. Then place the disc in the palm of your hand and form a depression by pressing the thumb of the other hand into the dough and twisting slightly. Repeat with all remaining dough to make orecchiette.

04

Venison ragout
Season the meat on all sides with salt and pepper. Heat a thin layer of olive oil in a large sauté pan over heat. Sear the meat in a single layer just to color on one side but do not cook through (you may need to do this in batches).

Transfer the meat into a non-reactive container, such as Pyrex, and pour in the wines. Cover and marinate refrigerated overnight.

05

06

You can use dried orecchiette but be sure to boil a bit longer. The pasta should be cooked a little bit more than al dente, but still hold its shape and have a bit of chew.

Remove the meat from the marinade and pat dry, reserving the marinade. Pass the meat through the coarse grind dye on a chilled meat grinder. Toss the ground meat with salt, freshly ground white pepper, and cloves.

07

Heat a thin layer of olive oil in a large Dutch oven or heavy bottomed saucepan over high heat. Add the ground meat and sear until caramelized and golden brown. Add the celery, carrots, onions, and garlic and cook, stirring, for 2 to 3 minutes. Stir in the tomato purée, season with salt and pepper, and mix well. Add the sage, rosemary, and red pepper flakes and continue to cook, while stirring, for 2 to 3 minutes.

08

Add the reserved marinade and simmer until the liquid has reduced by half. Add the veal stock and simmer over low heat, stirring constantly, until the liquid has reduced by half. Stir in the milk, heavy cream, and Parmesan cheese; season to taste with salt and freshly ground white pepper. Keep warm.

09

Vegetables and chestnuts
Heat the olive oil in a large skillet over medium-high heat. Add the mushrooms, chestnuts, and squash to the pan. Season with salt and pepper, and cook until tender and golden brown, 8 to 10 minutes. Add a splash of veal stock and cook for one more minute.

Combine with the venison ragout. Bring a large pot of salted water to a boil. Add the orecchiette and cook for 6 minutes, or until tender. Strain, add to the ragout with the parsley leaves, stir to coat. Serve ragout and pasta topped with shaved Parmesan and crispy sage leaves.

10

11

SEA BASS
"EN PAUPIETTE"

I'm taking you back twenty-six years to my early days as chef at the famed Le Cirque in New York City—to the site where restaurant DANIEL is housed today. This dish was created using four main ingredients—sea bass, leek, potato, and red wine. The original recipe is now served only at Café Boulud, while every year at DANIEL we create a new recipe around the same four elements, but with new techniques and presentations.

The art of any classic dish that we remember from a great chef is that it is composed of fairly simple elements. In this recipe, the trick is in the special technique of overlapping translucent sheets of potato, which requires the large Idaho variety sliced very thinly—either with a turning slicer or mandoline—to wrap around the sea bass. By the time you roast the potatoes crispy on all sides, the fish is perfectly cooked. I also add a *pomme purée* to offer a contrasting texture of potato.

This is my interpretation of fish and chips—more elegant, with a real Lyonnais slant.

RECEIPE

SERVES 6 - Preparation time: 1 hour - Cooking time: 30 minutes

DRINK PAIRING

A Syrah based wine such as Cornas or St. Joseph

PAUPIETTE

- ❒ 6 boneless, skinless sea bass fillets, 7 ounces each (200 g)
- ❒ Canola oil for frying
- ❒ 2 very large Idaho baking potatoes, peeled
- ❒ Salt and freshly ground white pepper

SAUCE MEURETTE

- ❒ ½ bottle red wine (375 ml)
- ❒ ½ cup ruby port (120 ml)
- ❒ ½ cup shallots, peeled and sliced (40 g)
- ❒ ½ teaspoon cracked black pepper (1 g)
- ❒ 1 sprig thyme
- ❒ 1 cup white veal stock (240 ml, see p. 109)
- ❒ ½ lb cold, unsalted butter cut into small pieces (225 g)
- ❒ Salt and freshly ground white pepper

POMME PURÉE

- ❒ 1 ½ pound peeled Yukon gold potatoes (680 g)
- ❒ 1 pint heavy cream (480 ml)
- ❒ 1 sprig fresh thyme
- ❒ 2 tablespoons butter (28 g)
- ❒ Salt and freshly ground white pepper

LEEKS

- ❒ 4 large leeks, two sliced and rinsed, and two cut into ½-inch (1.25-cm) dice

(spinach column)

- ❒ 2 cups packed spinach, washed and stemmed (40 g)
- ❒ 2 tablespoons butter (28 g)
- ❒ 6 baby leeks or scallions, each cut into a 4-inch (10-cm) baton from the stem end
- ❒ Sugar
- ❒ Salt and freshly ground white pepper

FINISH

- ❒ 2 tablespoons clarified butter (30 ml)
- ❒ Fleur de sel

Paupiette

Make each fillet as rectangular as possible (about 5 x 2 inch—12.75 x 5 cm) by slicing horizontally through 1-inch (2.5 cm) of the thick end of the fillet and folding it over toward the thinner side to flatten the surface.

01

Cut a vertical score on the tail end of each fillet, a few inches from the end, making sure not to cut all the way through, and tuck that end under.

02

Fill ⅓ of a heavy bottomed sauce pan with oil and heat to 250°F (120°C). Slice potatoes into long sheets on a Japanese turning slicer (or mandoline) and cut sheets into at least 36 rectangles, 1-inch (2.5 cm) wide by 6 inch (20 cm) long.

Fry potatoes until cooked and translucent but not colored. Drain onto a parchment paper-lined tray in a single layer and let cool at room temperature. Line up 6-7 slices of potato with the long ends overlapping by ¼-inch (0.5 cm) to reach the length of a portion of fish. Repeat with remaining potatoes to make 5 more portions and store sheets in between pieces of parchment paper.

If you don't have a Japanese turning slicer, you can slice the potatoes on a mandoline, and use two 4-inch-(10-cm) long sheets of potato per row.

Up to 6 hours before serving, season fish on all sides with salt and pepper and place 1 portion in the center of a potato sheet. Wrap one side of potato over the fish, and then tightly wrap the other side over the top, overlapping by ¼-inch (0.5 cm). Repeat with remaining 5 portions and store fish wrapped in parchment paper.

05

Sauce Meurette

In a large saucepan, combine the red wine, port, shallots, cracked pepper, and thyme and simmer until reduced to 1 cup (240 ml). Add stock and reduce by half. Strain through a fine-mesh sieve.

06

When ready to serve, bring to a simmer, remove from the heat and whisk in butter a few pieces at a time, just until melted. Season with salt and pepper.

Pomme purée

Place potatoes in a large saucepan and cover with cold salted water. Bring to a simmer and cook until tender. Meanwhile, in a small saucepan, simmer the cream with the thyme until reduced by half. Add butter, stir to melt, remove the thyme, and keep warm. Strain the water from the potatoes and return to the pan over medium heat, stirring until potatoes are dry. Pass potatoes through a food mill, return to a clean saucepan over low heat, and whisk in the cream mixture until well combined. Season to taste and keep warm.

08

After adding butter to the sauce, do not bring back to a simmer, as it will break. If it does, remove from the heat and whisk in a splash of cold water to bring it back together.

Leek and spinach purée

Bring a large pot of salted water to a boil and place a bowl of ice water on the side. Boil the two sliced leeks and spinach until very tender, and then chill in the ice water.

Transfer the leeks and spinach to a blender and purée with enough ice water to make a smooth, thick purée. Pass through a fine-mesh sieve.

09

10

Diced leeks

When ready to serve, divide the butter into two medium sauté pans and warm over medium heat. Add the 2 diced leeks to one pan and baby leeks to the other, along with a pinch of sugar and a splash of water. Cook, stirring occasionally until soft, about 6 to 8 minutes. Add leek purée to the diced leeks and season to taste both preparations with salt and pepper. Keep warm.

11

Fish

Melt the clarified butter in a large nonstick pan over medium-high heat. Carefully add the bass, and sear, undisturbed on one side until golden brown, about 3 to 4 minutes. Delicately turn over, and sear the other side for 3 to 4 more minutes or until golden. Let the fish rest for one minute.

Plating

For each serving, place a spoonful of pomme purée on the bottom of a warm dinner plate. Place a spoonful of leeks with purée in the center of the potatoes. Top with a piece of fish and a baby leek. Spoon sauce around the bass and sprinkle the fish with some fleur de sel.

CEDAR-GRILLED ROUGET
FENNEL AND MUSHROOM FILLING, LEMON VINAIGRETTE

This is a sensual dish that evokes the romance of the south of France. In the summertime, I picture playing pétanque with my buddies, sipping Ricard on the Côte d'Azur—dreaming of the fennel, licorice, and anise flavors I love. But this dish is also an homage to one of my mentors, Roger Vergé, and my time as a young chef at his restaurant Moulin de Mougins, where I cooked many red mullet, known as rouget.

Rouget is one of the most delicate, prized and appreciated fish of the Mediterranean, often grilled or used in bouillabaisse. The idea here is to stuff it with fennel, mushroom, and lemon, and to accentuate the flavor with lemon zest, fennel pollen, and Espelette pepper. Cooking it with the cedar sheets has two benefits: it helps hold the stuffed fillets together and gives a wonderful oaky flavor while grilling.

RECIPE

Serves 6 - Preparation time: 1 hour - Cooking time: 15 minutes

DRINK PAIRING

Provence white such as Château Simone

CEDAR WRAPPED ROUGET

- ❏ 6 whole rouget, approximately 1 lb each (455 g)
- ❏ 1 bulb fennel, with stems
- ❏ 6 bulbs baby fennel
- ❏ 4 tablespoons olive oil (60 ml)
- ❏ 3 cloves garlic, minced
- ❏ Salt and freshly ground white pepper
- ❏ 2 tablespoons Pernod Ricard (30 ml)
- ❏ 8 ounces button mushrooms, sliced (230 g)
- ❏ Espelette pepper, as needed
- ❏ Fennel pollen, as needed
- ❏ Zest and juice of 1 lemon
- ❏ 4 sheets cedar paper, soaked in water overnight

VINAIGRETTE

- ❏ ¼ teaspoon fennel pollen (0.5 g)
- ❏ 1 ½ tablespoons minced shallot (12 g)
- ❏ Zest and juice of 1 lemon
- ❏ ⅓ cup olive oil (80 ml)
- ❏ 1 tablespoon white balsamic vinegar (15 ml)
- ❏ Salt and freshly ground white pepper
- ❏ Espelette pepper

GARNISH AND PLATING

- ❏ ¼ cup fennel fronds, reserved from above (4 g)
- ❏ 1 head frisée lettuce, trimmed and washed
- ❏ Salt and freshly ground white pepper

Filling

Pick ¼ cup of the fennel fronds for salad. Discard stalks. With a mandoline, thinly slice 12 ounces (360 g) of the fennel bulb and set aside. Slice the baby fennel lengthwise on the mandoline and keep in ice water.

01

In a large sauté pan over medium-low heat, heat 2 tablespoons (30 ml) of the olive oil. Add the sliced fennel bulb and garlic and sprinkle with salt and pepper. Cook, stirring occasionally until the fennel is tender. Add the Pernod and flambé. Transfer to a bowl.

02

If you can't find fennel pollen, you may substitute toasted and finely ground fennel seed.

Add the remaining oil to the pan and place over high heat. Once very hot, add the sliced mushrooms and sear, undisturbed for 1 minute. Toss and continue to sear until the mushrooms are tender. Season to taste with salt and pepper and transfer to the bowl with the fennel.

Rouget

Fillet the rouget and remove pin bones, leaving the skin on.

Place 3 fillets skin side down on a sheet of plastic wrap and season with salt, pepper, Espelette, and fennel pollen.

Zest the lemon over top. Stir the lemon juice into the filling. Spoon approximately ¼ cup filling onto the fillets. Wrap tightly in the plastic wrap, tying the ends taught, and repeat to make 4 logs. Refrigerate for at least 1 hour.

04   **05**

Cut the plastic from the ends of the rougets and carefully unwrap. Generously brush the cedar paper with olive oil and tighty wrap around the rouget logs; trimming excess paper. Tie logs 3 times with butcher's twine. Brush the outside of the paper with olive oil.

06

Heat grill pan to medium-high heat. Sear logs on all sides for about 6 minutes total, or until fish is cooked and filling is hot. Unwrap the fish from the cedar paper, reserving it for presentation.

07

You can check the doneness of the fish by inserting a cake tester in the center for a few seconds and pressing it to your bottom lip to see if it is warm. When the filling is warm, the fish is cooked.
You could substitute other small fish such as trout.

Vinaigrette

In a small bowl, whisk to combine ingredients, seasoning to taste with salt, pepper, and Espelette.

Plating

In a medium bowl, toss the sliced baby fennel, fennel fronds, and frisée with the vinaigrette, salt, and pepper to taste. Present the rouget on the cedar paper, top with salad, and drizzle vinaigrette around.

MOROCCAN CHICKEN TAGINE
WITH CAULIFLOWER

Tagine is one of the most soulful dishes of Northwest Africa and refers to both the food itself and the vessel in which it is often cooked and served. The most classic tagines are made with lamb, chicken, goat, and vegetables, and the delicate and tangy flavors that the region is known for are expressed in this quintessential Berber dish.

What's wonderful about my Moroccan-inspired tagine is that the spices bring a delicious, warm finish, rather than a hot and spicy one. Tagine is one of the great recipes where everything is cooked together and both meat and vegetables get equal attention.

Create a mix of toasty spices using a mortar and pestle to grind everything together for a blend that lends an exotic finish. Briny olives and preserved lemon add complexity and contrast to the earthy notes of saffron, cardamom, cinnamon, sweet paprika, and coriander, creating a harmonious combination.

RECERE

DRINK PAIRING
Bandol rosé or a white Rioja

SPICE MIX (MAKES EXTRA)

- ❏ 7 tablespoons sweet paprika (48 g)
- ❏ 2 teaspoons garlic powder (5 g)
- ❏ 4 - 5 cinnamon sticks (17.5 g)
- ❏ 6 ¼ tablespoons coriander seeds (25 g)

- ❏ 2 tablespoons + 1 teaspoon ground turmeric (20 g)
- ❏ 2 tablespoons ginger powder (12.5 g)
- ❏ 1 teaspoon ground nutmeg (2.5 g)
- ❏ ½ tablespoon cardamom pods (2.5 g)
- ❏ 1 tablespoon + ½ teaspoon ground allspice (12.5 g)

CHICKEN TAGINE

- ❏ 1 farm-raised chicken
- ❏ 2 tablespoons spice mix (11 g) + extra for sauce
- ❏ ⅓ cup olive oil (80 ml)
- ❏ 1 head cauliflower
- ❏ 3 Roma tomatoes
- ❏ 1 large onion, diced
- ❏ 3 cloves garlic, minced
- ❏ 1 tablespoon grated ginger (24 g)

- ❏ 1 pinch saffron
- ❏ ¼ teaspoon spice mix (0.5 g)
- ❏ 1 tablespoon tomato paste (16 g)
- ❏ 2 cups chicken stock (480 ml, see p. 108)
- ❏ 3 tablespoons preserved lemon confit rind (approximately 2 lemons)
- ❏ 1 cup Castelvetrano olives (150 g)
- ❏ 1 bunch cilantro, leaves picked

Spice mix

In a large dry sauté pan, toast the spices over low heat. Transfer to a mortar and pestle and grind until well combined. Store in a dry, covered container.

01

Chicken tagine

Butcher the chicken into breasts, legs, and thighs. Remove the bones from the thighs and the wing tips from the breasts. Season the chicken on all sides with 2 tablespoons (11 g) of the spice mix and 3 tablespoons (45 ml) of the olive oil. Save all the bones for the chicken stock (see p. 108).

02

You could also use a clean, handheld coffee grinder to blend your spices.

Cauliflower and tomatoes
Trim the cauliflower into bite-sized florets.

03

Core the tomatoes and score an "x" on the bottoms. Bring a large pot of salted water to a boil and set a bowl of ice water on the side. Boil the cauliflower florets for 3 minutes and then submerge in the ice water. When chilled, drain and pat dry. Boil the tomatoes for 20 seconds, chill in the ice water, and peel the skins. Cut into quarters lengthwise and trim away the seeds to make petals.

Preheat oven to 350°F (175°C). Heat the remaining olive oil in a large sauté pan over medium heat. Sear the chicken, starting skin-side down until lightly browned (you may need to do this in batches), and then transfer to a tagine or 5-quart Dutch oven. In the same sauté pan, sear the cauliflower until golden and transfer to the tagine with the chicken.

05

Reduce the heat of the sauté pan to medium-low heat, add the onion, garlic, ginger, saffron, and spice mix. Cook, stirring for 3 to 4 minutes or until onions are translucent.

06

Add the tomato paste and chicken stock, and simmer until reduced by ⅓.

07

Pour sauce into the tagine over the chicken. Cover, and transfer to the oven for 20 minutes. Remove, stir in the tomatoes, preserved lemon rind, and olives, re-cover and cook for 20 more minutes or until the chicken is cooked through. Serve chicken in the tagine and garnish with cilantro leaves.

This dish is great served with a semolina couscous or fragrant basmati rice.

HARISSA-SPICED LAMB
EGGPLANT AND M'HAMSA COUSCOUS

Here we are with the warm flavors of the Middle East and eastern Mediterranean in a dish that takes you to the kebab shops in the souks of Istanbul, where wonderful aromas of grilled, spiced meat greet you.

The contrast in the recipe is in the double textures of eggplant— one that is roasted in the oven and blended with spice, olive oil, and lemon; and the other, which gets caramelized with honey and sherry vinegar for a bright, powerful aigre doux glaze. The large pearl couscous is the perfect bed to set the lamb, and absorb its juices.

There are sweet, tangy, and roasted notes here, perfectly complemented with a refreshing dressing of yogurt, cucumber, and mint.

RECITE

DRINK PAIRING

Full, bodied Southern Rhone such as Gigondas

SPICED LAMB LOIN

- ❏ 1 lamb saddle, trimmed into 2 loins and 2 tenderloins
- ❏ 1 tablespoon + 2 teaspoons harissa spice mix (8.5 g, Le Sanctuaire)
- ❏ Grapeseed oil, as needed
- ❏ 1 teaspoon dried mint (1 g)
- ❏ 1 teaspoon dried parsley (1 g)

EGGPLANT PURÉE AND GLAZED EGGPLANT

- ❏ 4 large eggplants
- ❏ Olive oil, as needed
- ❏ Salt and freshly ground white pepper
- ❏ 1 shallot, sliced
- ❏ 2 cloves garlic, sliced
- ❏ 1 teaspoon harissa spice mix (1.5 g, Le Sanctuaire)
- ❏ Juice of 1 lemon
- ❏ ¼ cup sherry vinegar (60 ml)
- ❏ 2 tablespoons honey (42 g)

M'HAMSA COUSCOUS

- ❏ 2 pints m'hamsa couscous (1 l)
- ❏ 2 tablespoons olive oil (30 ml)
- ❏ 4 cloves of garlic, chopped
- ❏ 2 pints chicken stock (0.95 l, see p. 108)
- ❏ 2 pinches harissa spice mix (Le Sanctuaire)
- ❏ Salt and freshly ground white pepper

YOGURT SAUCE

- ❏ 2 cups thick Greek yogurt (480 g)
- ❏ 1 cup peeled, seeded, and grated cucumber (200 g)
- ❏ 4 cloves garlic, peeled, germ removed, and finely grated
- ❏ Zest of 1 lemon, freshly grated
- ❏ 4 tablespoons fresh chopped mint (8 g)
- ❏ Salt and freshly ground white pepper

GARNISH AND PLATING

- ❏ Fleur de sel
- ❏ A few small pieces lavash cracker (see p. 109)
- ❏ ½ cup mint leaves

Lamb

Combine harissa spice mix and dried herbs with enough grapeseed oil to make a slurry. Brush onto the lamb and refrigerate overnight.

01

Eggplant purée

Preheat the oven to 350°F (175°C). Slice 2 eggplants in half lengthwise and rub with olive oil, sprinkle with salt and pepper.

02

The main components of this dish can also be made as a kebab with other more affordable cuts of lamb such as leg or shoulder.

Transfer to a baking sheet lined with aluminium foil, cut side down, and bake for 25 minutes, or until very tender. Remove from the oven, and when cool enough to handle, scrape away the flesh, and discard the skin.

03

Heat a thin layer of olive oil in a medium saucepan over medium heat and add the shallot and garlic. Sweat for 2 minutes, or until translucent, then add the cooked eggplant and spice mix. Cook for another 5 minutes or until the spices smell toasted.

04

Transfer contents to a blender. Purée with lemon juice and enough olive oil to make a smooth purée. Season to taste with salt and pepper.

05

Glazed eggplant
Slice remaining eggplants lengthwise into ½-inch (1.25 cm) thick slices.

06

Cut slices into at least 32 rectangles about 3-inch (7.5 cm) long and 1-inch (2.5 cm) wide. With a small knife, lightly score the flesh on both sides of the eggplant slices in a crosshatch pattern and season on both sides with salt and pepper.

Heat a thin layer of olive oil in a large sauté pan over high heat. Add eggplant in a single layer (you may need to do this in batches) and sear until golden brown on both sides, about 1 minute each. Reduce heat to medium and add the sherry vinegar and honey. Bring to a simmer until reduced to a glaze. Set aside and repeat with remaining eggplant.

Couscous – Heat the olive oil in a medium saucepan over medium heat. Add the garlic and cook, stirring until translucent. Add the chicken stock and bring to a boil. Stir in the couscous and spice and return to a boil.

Remove from the stove and cover with a lid. Rest for 7 minutes, and then fluff with a fork. Season to taste with salt and pepper.

09
10

Yogurt sauce

Toss the grated cucumber with 1 teaspoon of salt (6 g), and rest at room temperature for 10 minutes to extract the liquid. Squeeze dry and transfer to a small bowl, combine all ingredients and season to taste. Reserve, chilled until ready to serve.

11

Pre-salting and straining the cucumber for the mint sauce will prevent the juices from weeping into the yogurt.

Lamb

When ready to serve, preheat a grill to medium-high heat. Grill the lamb on all sides to medium rare, about 5 to 8 minutes (130°F or 54.5°C). Remove from the grill and rest for 5 minutes before slicing.

12

For each serving, spread a spoonful of eggplant purée on the bottom of a plate. Place a spoonful of couscous adjacent, top with 4 pieces of the glazed eggplant and set sliced lamb on top. Sprinkle the lamb with fleur de sel. Scoop a spoonful of yogurt sauce onto the lamb, place a lavash cracker and sprig of mint on top.

13

PALERON CARBONNADE
WITH BRAISED ENDIVE

This paleron carbonnade, a classic Belgian preparation, was introduced to our menus by an authentic Belgian— our corporate chef Fabrizio Salerni. Paleron, known in America as flat-iron steak, is a very good cut to braise and will serve a large group of people.

This dish is about the rustic, classic *cuisine du Nord*, which we celebrate at Bar Boulud, our wine bar and bistro where we love to serve old-fashioned hearty dishes. The complexity comes from the Chimay beer—a dark Trappist beer with tones of molasses— we use and also from the sweet, spiced gingerbread which acts as a liaison between the sauce and the meat, bringing depth and wonderful unctuosity. The slight bitterness of the Belgian endive, or witloof, cuts through the richness of the sauce and the glazed root vegetables become like treasures in the dish, adding new layers and textures.

RECURSE

SERVES 8 - Preparation time: 1 hour - Cooking time: 3 hours

DRINK PAIRING

Structured Saint-Emilion or Côtes de Castillon

PALERON CARBONNADE

- ❏ 5 pounds beef paleron, trimmed of all fat (2.3 kg)
- ❏ Salt and ground black pepper
- ❏ 2 tablespoons extra-virgin olive oil (30 ml)
- ❏ 3 medium onions, sliced
- ❏ 2 branches celery, thinly sliced

- ❏ 1 large carrot, peeled and thinly sliced
- ❏ 2 garlic cloves, thinly sliced
- ❏ 1 bouquet garni (2 sprigs thyme, parsley stems, 2 bay leaves, tied with butcher's twine)
- ❏ ¼ teaspoon crushed black pepper
- ❏ 4 bottles (33 cl each) Chimay beer

- ❏ 2 tablespoons red wine vinegar (30 ml)
- ❏ ¼ cup Dijon mustard (60 g)
- ❏ 3 cups veal stock (720 ml, see p. 109)
- ❏ ½ cup gingerbread (25 g) cut into ½-inch cubes
- ❏ ¼ cup fresh flat-leaf parsley leaves (4 g)

BRAISED ENDIVE

- ❏ 4 Belgian endives, halved lengthwise
- ❏ 2 tablespoons butter (28 g)
- ❏ Salt and freshly ground white pepper
- ❏ 2 large carrots, cut in 16 ¼-inch (0.75 cm) thick slices (0.5 g)
- ❏ 16 baby turnips, halved
- ❏ 16 red pearl onions, peeled
- ❏ 2 cups veal stock (480 ml, see p. 109)

78

Paleron

Center a rack in the oven and preheat to 300°F (150°C). Season the beef on all sides with salt and ground black pepper. In a large cast-iron pot, or Dutch oven, over high heat, warm the olive oil. Add the beef to the pot and sear until dark golden brown on all sides, 20 to 25 minutes. Remove the beef from the pot and reserve.

01

Add the onions, celery, and carrot and cook, stirring, until they turn a deep, caramel color, about 20 minutes. Add the garlic, bouquet garni, and black pepper.

02

Add the beer and vinegar and bring to a simmer, scraping up any browned bits that stick to the bottom of the pan. Whisk in the Dijon mustard. Return the beef to the pot and add 3 cups of veal stock (720 ml).

Add the gingerbread and bring to a simmer. Cover the pot and transfer it to the oven. Braise until the meat is tender, about 3 hours, turning the meat once or twice.

If you can't find Belgian Chimay beer, New York State's Ommegang Brewery's Abbey Ale is a close substitute.

Remove the beef, and when cool enough to handle, slice into 8 portions. Strain the sauce through a chinois and press well. If needed, reduce the sauce until thick enough to coat the back of a spoon.

05

Place beef slices in a baking dish, coat with sauce, and place in oven to heat through.

06

You can prepare the braise up to three days in advance.

Endives

Brown the butter in a large sauté pan or baking dish. Season endives with salt and pepper and sear cut side down until browned.

07

Turn over and add the carrots, turnips, onions, and veal stock and bring to a simmer. Cover, and transfer to the oven. Bake for 20 minutes, or until vegetables are tender. Remove, and if needed return to the stove to reduce the liquid to a glaze.

For each serving, place a piece of paleron carbonnade in a wide bowl, cover with sauce and top with a piece of braised endive. Place 2 each of the carrots, red pearl onions, and baby turnips around and garnish with parsley leaves.

Your gingerbread should taste more spiced than sweet.

GÂTEAU BASQUE
WITH BRANDIED CHERRIES, VANILLA CRÈME ANGLAISE

When I was fifteen, and worked a summer at Hotel Etchola in the small village of Ascain in the Pyrenees of the Basque Country, I had my first taste of Gâteau Basque. Then it was still a truly local specialty in the southwest, which you couldn't find in Lyon or New York City!

This now-iconic torte served at Bar Boulud in New York and London has a very thick, custardy filling that's encased in a shell of buttery dough made with granulated sugar and almond flour to lend a bit of crunch.

The classic way to prepare it is to bake black cherry jam in the custard, but we prefer to serve brandied cherries on the side along with crème anglaise and crème fraîche chantilly. Putting a touch of cherry liqueur in the filling is a nice way to maintain the DNA of this homey comfort food while adding a modern spin.

RECESS

DRINK PAIRING
Sauternes, Barsac, or Sainte-Croix-du-Mont

DOUGH

- ❏ 4 ½ ounces butter, at room temperature (130 g)
- ❏ 1 cup sugar (205 g)
- ❏ 2 egg yolks (20 g each)
- ❏ 1 egg (50 g)
- ❏ ¼ teaspoon lemon oil (1 g)
- ❏ ¾ tablespoons baking powder (10 g)

- ❏ ¾ teaspoons salt (4,5 g)
- ❏ 1 ½ cups + 2 tablespoons flour (210 g)
- ❏ ½ cup almond flour (60 g)
- ❏ 1 egg, beaten with 1 tablespoon of milk

VANILLA PASTRY CREAM

- ❏ 1 vanilla bean

- ❏ ½ cup + 2 tablespoons sugar (124 g)
- ❏ 6 egg yolks (120 g)
- ❏ 1 egg (50 g)
- ❏ 3 ½ tablespoons flour (30 g)
- ❏ ¼ cup cornstarch (38 g)
- ❏ 2 ¼ cups milk (540 ml)
- ❏ 1 tablespoon Kirsch (15 ml)

CRÈME CHANTILLY

- ❏ 1 cup crème fraîche (240 g)
- ❏ 3 tablespoons heavy cream (45 ml)
- ❏ 2 tablespoons sugar (24 g)

GARNISH AND PLATING

- ❏ Vanilla crème anglaise (see p. 109)
- ❏ ½ cup brandied cherries (120 g, optional)

Dough

In a stand mixer fitted with the paddle attachment, mix together the butter and sugar until soft and airy. Add the egg yolks, egg, and lemon oil and mix until incorporated.

01

In a small bowl, whisk together the baking powder, salt, and flour and slowly add into the butter mixture. Add the almond flour and mix until fully incorporated. Remove the dough and form into two flat disks. Wrap in plastic and refrigerate at least 2 hours, or overnight.

02

Pastry cream

Using a small knife, slice the vanilla bean in half lengthwise and scrape out the seeds.

In a medium bowl, whisk to combine sugar, egg yolks, and egg, and then gradually whisk in the flour and cornstarch.

In a small saucepan, bring the milk and vanilla bean seeds to a boil, then remove from the heat.

05

Carefully pour about ½ cup (120 ml) of the hot milk into the egg mixture, whisking constantly. Whisk the milk and egg mixture into the remaining hot milk in the saucepan.

06

Return to low heat and cook, whisking, until thickened (like pudding) and the consistency gets smooth and shiny, about 4 to 5 minutes total.

Remove from heat and pour into a bowl. Stir in the kirsch. Cool to room temperature with a thin layer of plastic wrap pressed on top, store in the refrigerator.

Assembling the tart

Preheat oven to 350°F (175°C) and place rack in center. Roll both discs of dough into rounds about 8 ½-inch (24 cm) in diameter and ¼-inch thick (0.5 cm). Chill until firm. Using your fingers, press one disc of dough evenly into the tart mold with a removable bottom, and trim excess.

09

Fill tart shell with the pastry cream and smooth the top.

10

To have a perfect fit, cut your chilled, rolled out dough only 1 cm- diameter wider than your ring mold to avoid overlapping on the sides.

Place the remaining dough on top. Use a rolling pin to seal the edges by rolling it accross the top of the mold, and trim away excess. Brush the top of the tart with the beaten egg.

11

Make a decorative pattern on the surface of the dough using the tines of a fork, drawing it across the surface at acute angles to achieve a diamond pattern. Bake for 35 minutes, or until golden brown. Cool on a rack. **Crème chantilly:** in a stand mixer or medium bowl, whisk all ingredients together to reach hard peaks. Keep chilled. Serve gâteau basque at room temperature with crème anglaise, a few brandied cherries, and crème chantilly.

12

Transfer the gâteau basque to a rack after baking and remove it from the mold before completely cooling to keep the dough crispy.

GRAPEFRUIT GIVRÉ
SESAME HALVA, ROSE LOUKOUM

Before opening Boulud Sud, I was inspired by the flavors of a trip to Turkey and asked Ghaya Oliveira, my pastry chef who created this dish, to capture all the wonders of the Turkish Mediterranean while paying homage to her Tunisian heritage.

Ghaya chose to hollow the frozen shell of a grapefruit, rather than a givré's traditional orange, and fill it with flavors and textures expressed in the cuisines of North Africa, Turkey, and the Middle East: delicate rosewater loukoum, grapefruit jam, sesame in many forms—tahini crumble, halva floss, sesame mousse, and a crispy tuile.

I find the grapefruit perfectly matches the light flavor of rosewater, and its acidity cuts through the sweetness of halva. The pleasure here is to discover the layers of flavors and textures as you dig into the sesame crumble, the mousse, and the sugar floss that is rolled in nutty sesame powder.

Ghaya is now the pastry chef at restaurant DANIEL but this dessert became an instant classic at Boulud Sud, and no one ever eats there without ordering it!

DRINK PAIRING
A Mosel Riesling Beerenauslese

- ☐ 7 ruby red grapefruits

ROSE LOUKOUM

- ☐ 6 sheets gelatin (14 g)
- ☐ 1 tablespoon grapefruit juice (14 g)
- ☐ 1 ¾ cups sugar (350 g)
- ☐ 4 tablespoons cornstarch, plus extra as needed (32 g)
- ☐ 1 pinch cream of tartar
- ☐ 2 teaspoons rose water (13 g)
- ☐ Pink food coloring, as needed

CITRUS TUILE

- ☐ ½ cup sugar (100 g)
- ☐ ¼ cup orange juice (60 ml)
- ☐ ¼ cup flour, sifted (32 g)
- ☐ 2 ounces butter, melted (56 g)

GRAPEFRUIT JAM

- ☐ ¾ cup + 3 tablespoons sugar (40 g)
- ☐ ¾ teaspoon apple pectin (1.5 g)
- ☐ 1 ¼ chopped grapefruit (260 g)

HALVA CRUMBLE

- ☐ ½ cup almond powder (50 g)
- ☐ ½ cup flour (64 g)
- ☐ 3 tablespoons halva paste (45 g)
- ☐ ¼ cup packed light brown sugar (50 g)
- ☐ 4 tablespoons room temperature butter (50 g)

SESAME FOAM

- ☐ 1 ½ sheets gelatin (3 g)
- ☐ 1 cup + 2 tablespoons heavy cream (245 g)
- ☐ ½ cup milk (120 ml)
- ☐ 3 tablespoons sesame paste (48 g)
- ☐ 2 tablespoons + 2 teaspoons sugar (38 g)
- ☐ ½ cup crème fraîche (115 g)

FINISH

- ☐ Grapefruit sorbet (see p. 108)
- ☐ 1 ½ cups halva candy floss (36 g)
- ☐ 1 tablespoon black sesame seeds (6 g)
- ☐ 1 tablespoon white sesame seeds (11 g)
- ☐ ¼ cup rose buds (11 g)

Grapefruits

Cut caps from 6 of the grapefruits. Hollow them out by running It in between the flesh and pith over a colander on top of a medium bowl.

01

Chop and reserve 1¼ cups (about 3 grapefruits) of the segments for jam. Measure 2 ½ cups juice (600 ml) for sorbet and 1 tablespoon for rose loukoum. Finely grate and reserve the zest of the 7th grapefruit for sorbet. Then, cut away the skin and cut out supremes, and dice them for finishing.

02

The hollowed grapefruit shells can be made in advance and kept in the freezer, wrapped in plastic.

Rose loukoum

Soak the gelatin sheets in ice water for 10 minutes; squeeze dry. In a small saucepan, simmer the grapefruit juice with 3 tablespoons water and sugar until it reaches 230°F (110°C).

In a small bowl, mix cornstarch with 2 tablespoons plus 2 teaspoons water (40 ml). Whisk the mixture into the saucepan and cook for 3 minutes, stirring. Add the soaked gelatin, cream of tartar, and rose water and stir in the food coloring until light pink-colored.

Spray a 5-6-inch (12.75-15.25 cm) square Pyrex with non-stick food spray and pour the mixture into the pan. Let cool at room temperature, remove from the pan, and cut into approximately ½-inch (1.25-cm) cubes. Toss the cubes in a bowl with a sprinkling of cornstarch to prevent sticking. Cover and store chilled.

05

Citrus tuile

In a bowl, whisk to combine the sugar, orange juice, and flour until smooth. Gradually whisk in the melted butter until homogenous. Chill overnight. Preheat oven to 325°F (175°C). Spread approximately 1 teaspoon batter (5 g) onto a Silpat-lined sheet tray into a 4-inch (10-cm) diameter round, thin stencil. Repeat to make at least 6 rounds, spaced 1-inch (2.5 cm) apart. Bake for 6 minutes, turning the tray 180 degrees halfway through, or until the tuiles are a lacy texture and are golden brown.

06

To help cut the loukoum and keep it from sticking, spray or rub your knife blade with a neutral cooking oil.

Halva crumble

Preheat oven to 350°F (175°C). In a large bowl with a dough cutter, combine all ingredients until well incorporated and the mixture forms large crumbs.

07

Sprinkle the dough onto a parchment paper—lined baking sheet in a single layer and bake for 5 minutes. Remove from the oven and with a bench scraper, chop the dough directly on the tray to break it into a small crumble. Return to the oven for 5 more minutes, or until golden brown. Cool at room temperature and store in a dry, airtight container.

Sesame foam

Soak the gelatin sheets in ice water for 10 minutes; squeeze dry. In a small saucepan, whisk to combine the cream, milk, sesame paste, and sugar and bring to a simmer.

09

Remove from the heat, stir in the soaked gelatin until dissolved, and chill by stirring over a bowl of ice. Once chilled, whisk in the crème fraîche. Transfer mixture to the canister of a whipped cream maker (or ISI foamer). Charge with two nitrogen cartridges, leaving the second one attached. Shake well. Store chilled.

10

Assembling

For each serving, place 2 scoops of sorbet in the bottom of a frozen grapefruit and spread to coat the inside walls. Add a spoonful of fresh grapefruit segments and a spoonful of grapefruit jam. Squeeze a dollop of sesame foam from the whipped cream maker on top of the grapefruit segments. Add about 3 pieces of rose loukoum.

11

Add a few pieces of halva crumble. Squeeze another dollop of foam on top. Cover with a citrus tuile and, using a torch, point the flame at the sides of the tuile without touching it, just to melt onto the rind, forming a cap. Top with a handful of halva floss and sprinkle with some sesame seeds. Repeat the process to make 6 givré. If desired, serve in a bowl of crushed ice decorated with rose buds.

12

GLOSSARY

GLOS SARY

AL DENTE
From Italian, literally means "to the tooth," when a grain or pasta is cooked so as to be firm when eaten.

BLANCH
To cook an ingredient in boiling water for a short period of time and then plunge into an ice-water bath to stop the cooking process.

BOLOGNESE
A meat-based sauce native to Bologna, Italy. Classic ingredients include onion, celery, and carrot, different types of finely chopped meat, wine, and a small amount of tomato concentrate and dairy.

CASTELVETRANO OLIVES
A DOC protected olive native to the region of Sicily in Italy, named after the town of Castelvetrano. They are large and green with a mild, buttery taste.

CEDAR PAPER
Flexible cedar sheets used to flavor foods that are being grilled. They must be thoroughly soaked before used to cook in order to avoid burning.

CHIFFONADE
A knife cut that produces fine strips or ribbons.

CLARIFIED BUTTER
Created by heating the butter so the milk solids and water separate from the butter fat.

COLZA OIL
From the same family as rapeseed oil. Obtained from the seeds of a plant that produces turnips.

CONCASSÉE
From the French word "concasser"—to crush or to grind. Tomato concassée is peeled, seeded, and finely diced.

FENNEL POLLEN
Golden powder harvested from fennel blossoms that have been dried, put through a separator, and sifted until fine.

FISH SAUCE
Also called "nam pla," a clear red-brown sauce often used in Thai cuisine, made from a blend of fish and salt which is fermented for at least one year.

GELATIN SHEET
An odorless, tasteless thickening agent that activates when combined with a heated liquid and then chilled.

GOLDEN MOUNTAIN SEASONING
A Thai sauce composed mainly of fermented soy beans, salt, and sugar.

HALVA

Meaning "dessert" or "sweets" in Arabic. Halva paste is made with ground sesame seeds and is similar in flavor to tahini. Halva floss is native to Turkey and is made from sugar and wheat flour into a consistency similar to cotton candy.

HARISSA

A brick-red spice, paste, or sauce-like condiment native to North Africa. Dried chilies are soaked, then pounded with garlic, caraway, and coriander seeds and sometimes mixed with oil.

JULIENNE

To cut ingredients into long, thin, match-like strips.

KIRSCH

Kirschwasser in German. It is a clear, colorless, sour—not sweet—fruit liqueur made from distilling cherries.

M'HAMSA COUSCOUS

Tunisian variety of coarse-grained whole wheat couscous with a unique texture and earthy, nutty taste. The grains are much larger and rounder than traditional fine couscous.

MARCONA ALMONDS

A round, sweet, and oily almond native to Spain.

MICROPLANE

Extremely fine graters used to grate different foods such as cheese or fruit zest.

ORLÉANS MUSTARD (MOUTARDE D'ORLÉANS)

Smooth and creamy mustard made from whole grain mustard seeds, Guérande salt, and Orléans vinegar.

PALERON

A French cut of beef from the shoulder, otherwise known as featherblade or flat-iron steak, best used for braising.

RED CURRY PASTE

A Thai cuisine staple made from a blend of red chilies, coriander roots and leaves, shrimp paste, lemongrass, garlic, shallots, and galangal.

SIFT

To put a fine, loose, or powdery substance through a sieve in order to remove lumps.

SRIRACHA SAUCE

Southeast-Asian hot sauce made from a paste of chili peppers, distilled vinegar, garlic, sugar, and salt. It is named after the coastal Thai city Si Racha.

SUPREME

To remove the skin and pith of a citrus fruit, and then cut between the membranes to separate it into segments.

THAI BIRD CHILI

Native to Southeast Asia, a very small and very hot pepper, either orange, red, or green. Hotter than a habanero chili pepper, with a fruity taste.

TOMATO PETALS

Peeled, seeded tomatoes cut into petal like shapes.

TRUMPET ROYALE

Also known as "king oyster" mushroom; it has a thick, meaty white stem and a small tan cap.

BASE RECIPES

CHICKEN STOCK
MAKES ABOUT 1 GALLON (3.8 L)

- 6 lbs chicken bones, wings, and/or trim, skinned, fat trimmed, rinsed, and patted dry (1.8 kg)
- 2 onions, peeled and cut into quarters
- 2 small carrots, peeled, and cut into 2-inch (5-cm) pieces
- 1 stalk celery, trimmed and cut into 2-inch (5-cm) pieces
- 1 medium leek, trimmed, split lengthwise, and rinsed
- 1 head garlic, split in half
- 1 bay leaf
- 5 sprigs parsley
- ½ teaspoon white peppercorns (1 g)

Put the chicken bones and 7 quarts (6.6 L) of cold water in a tall stockpot and bring to a rolling boil. Add another 3 quarts (2.8 l) very cold water and skim off the fat that rises to the top. Reduce the heat to a simmer and skim regularly for 10 minutes.

Add the remaining ingredients to the pot and simmer, uncovered, for 4 hours, continuing to skim. Drain the stock into a colander set over a bowl. Discard the solids, then pass the liquid through a fine-mesh sieve lined with cheesecloth, and discard the solids. Chill and store, covered, in the refrigerator for up to 1 week, or freeze and use as needed.

COURT BOUILLON
MAKES 1 GALLON (3.8 L)

- 5 tablespoons coarse sea salt (70 g)
- 4 tablespoons black peppercorns (24 g)
- 1 ½ tablespoons coriander seeds (10 g)
- 2 star anise
- 6 medium carrots, peeled and sliced
- 4 onions, peeled and sliced
- 1 head fennel, sliced
- 10 cloves garlic, peeled
- 1 (1-inch/2.5-cm) knob of ginger, peeled and sliced
- Peels and juice of 1 orange
- 1 bay leaf
- 2 basil stems
- 1 cup dry white wine (240 ml)
- ½ cup white vinegar (120 ml)

Pour 1 gallon of water into a large stockpot and add the salt, spices, vegetables, orange peel and juice, and herbs. Bring to a boil, then reduce the heat, cover, and simmer for 20 minutes. Add the white wine and vinegar, simmer for 5 more minutes, then strain through a fine-meshed sieve. Use immediately or chill over ice and store, covered and refrigerated, for up to 1 week.

CRISPY SAGE LEAVES
MAKES ABOUT 30

- Vegetable oil for frying
- 1 bunch fresh sage, leaves picked
- Salt

Fill a saucepan ⅓ with vegetable oil and heat to 325°F (163°C). In three batches, submerge the sage leaves and fry until bubbles subside but not browned (about 5 seconds). Strain onto a paper towel—lined plate and sprinkle with salt.
Cool and store in an airtight container up to 1 week.

GRAPEFRUIT SORBET
MAKES 1 1/2 PINTS (710 ML)

- ¾ cups water (180 ml)
- 1 cup sugar (200 g)
- 2 ½ cups ruby red grapefruit juice (600 ml, reserved from grapefruits)
- Finely grated zest from 1 pink grapefruit (see p. 98)

In a medium saucepan, combine the water and sugar and bring to a simmer until dissolved. Pour into a bowl set over ice and stir until well chilled. Add the grapefruit juice and zest and stir to combine.

Spin in an ice cream machine according to the manufacturer's instructions. Keep frozen.

LAVASH
MAKES ABOUT 12

- ❏ 1 ¾ cups all-purpose flour, plus more as needed (240 g)
- ❏ ½ teaspoon salt, plus more as needed (2 g)
- ❏ 1 teaspoon olive oil, plus more as needed (5 ml)
- ❏ ⅓ cup plain yogurt (75 g)
- ❏ ⅓ cup plus 1 teaspoon water (85ml)
- ❏ Dried sumac, as needed
- ❏ Za'atar spice, as needed

In a stand mixer fitted with a paddle attachment, mix the flour, salt, and then add the olive oil, yogurt, and water until the dough comes together. Knead on a floured surface for a few minutes until smooth. Wrap with plastic and refrigerate for at least 1 hour. Preheat a plancha or large skillet to high heat. Preheat oven to 275°F (135°C). Divide dough in 6. Roll dough by hand or through a pasta machine to a very thin sheet; slice the sheet in half. Sear dough sheets on both sides on the plancha just to lightly brown, and then transfer in a single layer to baking sheets lined with parchment paper. Brush

the top of the cracker with a thin layer of olive oil and sprinkle the surface with salt, sumac, and za'atar.

Transfer to the oven until browned and crisp, about 10 minutes.

VANILLA CRÈME ANGLAISE
MAKES 1 1/4 CUPS (300 ML)

- ❏ 1 cup heavy cream (210 g/240 ml)
- ❏ ½ vanilla bean, split and seeds scraped
- ❏ 3 egg yolks (20 g each)
- ❏ ¼ cup sugar (50 g)

In a medium saucepan, combine the cream and vanilla bean. In a medium bowl, whip the egg yolks and sugar until airy. Bring the cream to a simmer and carefully pour about ½ cup of the hot cream into the egg mixture, whisking constantly. Whisk the egg mixture into the remaining hot cream in the saucepan. Return to low heat and cook, whisking, until it reaches 183°F (84°C). Immediately strain into a bowl set over ice water. Stir until chilled.

VEAL STOCK
MAKES ABOUT 1 GALLON (3.8 L)

- ❏ 6 pounds veal bones, cut into 2-inch (5-cm) slices, fat trimmed, and rinsed (2.7 kg)
- ❏ 2 tablespoons vegetable oil (30 ml)
- ❏ 2 onions, peeled and quartered
- ❏ 2 small carrots, peeled and cut into 2-inch (5-cm) pieces
- ❏ 2 stalks celery, cut into 2-inch (5-cm) pieces
- ❏ 1 tablespoon tomato paste (16 g)
- ❏ 4 ounces button mushrooms, trimmed, cleaned, and halved (113 g)
- ❏ 6 cloves garlic, peeled and smashed
- ❏ 5 sprigs parsley
- ❏ 2 sprigs thyme
- ❏ 2 bay leaves
- ❏ ½ teaspoon white peppercorns (1 g)

Place the bones in a large stockpot and cover with cold water. Bring to a boil, then strain the bones and rinse them with cold water; wipe the stockpot clean. Meanwhile, in a large sauté pan, heat the oil over medium-high heat and add the onions, carrots, and celery. Cook, stirring, for 5 minutes, or until they start to caramelize. Add the tomato paste and cook, stirring, for 5 minutes; set aside. Return the bones to the pot, add 6 quarts cold water, and simmer for 10 minutes, skimming away any foam that rises to the surface. Add the cooked vegetables, the mushrooms, garlic, parsley, thyme, bay leaves, and peppercorns. Simmer, skimming as needed, for 4 hours. Strain the stock through a fine-mesh sieve lined with cheesecloth and discard the solids. Chill and store, covered, in the refrigerator for up to 1 week, or freeze and use as needed.

DANIEL BOULUD'S ADDRESS BOOK

WWW.DANIELBOULUD.COM

NEW YORK

DANIEL
60 EAST 65TH STREET
NEW YORK, NY 10065
TEL. 1 (212) 288-0033

CAFÉ BOULUD
20 E 76TH ST
NEW YORK, NY 10021
TEL. 1 (212) 772-2600

BAR BOULUD
1900 BROADWAY
NEW YORK, NY 10023
TEL. 1 (212) 595-0303

ÉPICERIE BOULUD
1900 BROADWAY
NEW YORK, NY 10023
TEL. 1 (212) 595-9606

DB BISTRO MODERNE
55 WEST 44TH ST #1
NEW YORK, NY 10036
TEL. 1 (212) 391-2400

BOULUD SUD
20 WEST 64TH ST
NEW YORK, NY 10023
TEL. 1 (212) 595-1313

DBGB
299 BOWERY
NEW YORK, NY 10003
TEL. 1 (212) 933-5300

MIAMI

DB BISTRO MODERNE
JW MARRIOT MARQUIS
255 BISCAYNE BOULEVARD WAY
MIAMI, FL 33131
TEL. 1 (305) 421-8800

PALM BEACH

CAFÉ BOULUD
THE BRAZILIAN COURT HOTEL
301 AUSTRALIAN AVENUE
PALM BEACH, FL 33480
TEL. 1 (561) 655-6060

DANIEL BOULUD'S ADDRESS BOOK

WWW.DANIELBOULUD.COM

BOSTON

BAR BOULUD
MANDARIN ORIENTAL BOSTON
776 BOYLSTON STREET
BOSTON, MA 02199
TEL. 1 (617) 535-8888

WASHINGTON DC

DBGB
CITYCENTER
931 H STREET NW
WASHINGTON, DC 20001

LAS VEGAS

DB BRASSERIE
THE VENETIAN RESORT
THE GRAND CANAL SHOPPES
3355 LAS VEGAS BOULEVARD SOUTH
LAS VEGAS, NY 89109
TEL. 1 (702) 430-1235

SINGAPORE

DB BISTRO MODERNE
THE SHOPPES AT MARINA BAY SANDS
B1-48, GALLERIA LEVEL
2 BAYFRONT AVENUE, SINGAPORE 018956
TEL. +65 6688 8525

CAFÉ BOULUD
FOUR SEASONS HOTEL
60 YORKVILLE AVE
TORONTO, ON M4W 0A4, CANADA
TEL. 1 (416) 963-6000

MAISON BOULUD
RITZ-CARLTON MONTREAL
1228 RUE SHERBROOKE OUEST
MONTREAL, QUÉBEC H3G 1H6, CANADA
TEL. 1 (514) 842-4224

BAR BOULUD
MANDARIN ORIENTAL HYDE PARK
66 KNIGHTSBRIDGE
LONDON SW1X 7LA,
UNITED KINGDOM
TEL. +44 20 7201 3899

PRODUCT INDEX

AJ SCHALLER

AJ Schaller has been working with Chef Daniel Boulud since 2004, and coordinated, tested, and prepared the dishes for this book. She is the Culinary Manager for the Dinex Group and directs recipe creation and editing for various publications.

MAISIE WILHELM

Maisie Wilhelm has worked with Chef Daniel Boulud since 2010 and is the co-author of this book. She started her career in journalism and now is Brand Manager for the Dinex Group, working on special projects.

THOMAS SCHAUER

Thomas Schauer has worked with Chef Daniel Boulud for more than a decade on several photographic adventures. One of the most renowned and talented food photographers, Thomas has worked with top chefs from around the world. He currently divides his time between Vienna and New York City.

115 West 18th Street
New York, NY 10011
www.abramsbooks.com

ACKNOWLEDGMENTS

These dishes were created with the collaboration of my corporate chefs Fabrizio Salerni, Olivier Muller, Eric Bertoïa; DANIEL executive chef Jean-François Bruel and chef de cuisine Eddy Leroux; executive chefs Gavin Kaysen, Aaron Chambers, Olivier Quignon, Travis Swikard, Charles Foster; executive pastry chefs Ghaya Oliveira and Tyler Atwell; head boulanger, Mark Fiorentino; and chef charcutier Aurelien Dufour.

Thank you also to Christine Doublet, Carla Siegel, and Lauren Young for their help, and a special thank-you to Lisa Callaghan from All-Clad for providing cookware for the photographs.

COLLECTION DIRECTOR
Emmanuel Jirou-Najou

EDITORIAL MANAGER
Alice Gouget

PHOTOGRAPHER
Thomas Schauer
Photo producer: Sahinaz Agamola-Schauer
Photo assistant: Alexander Lau

GRAPHIC DESIGN
Soins graphiques
Thanks to Sophie Brice

DRINK PAIRING
Daniel Johnnes

PHOTOENGRAVING
Nord Compo

MARKETING & COMMUNICATION MANAGER
Camille Gonnet
camille.gonnet@alain-ducasse.com

ISBN 978-2-84123-725-8
Legal Deposit : 4th quarter 2014
Printed in China
© Alain Ducasse Édition 2014
84, avenue Victor Cresson
92130 Issy-les-Moulineaux
France
http://www.alain-ducasse.com/en/livres-ebooks-applications

The editor thanks Bowery itchen, our exclusive supplier for this book.

COOK
WITH YOUR
FAVORITE
CHEFS

PIERRE HERMÉ · ALAIN **DUCASSE** · ERIC **RIPERT**

my BEST

ILLUSTRATED **COOKING COURSES** FROM **FINEST CHEFS**

TO HELP YOU PRODUCE THEIR **TOP 10 RECIPES** WITH

PERFECT RESULTS EVERY TIME!

ALAIN DUCASSE
PUBLISHING

www.alain-ducasse.com